11. 2071

— 50/0

# DANCING
# ON BONES

*Elizabeth Rapp*

# Dancing
# on Bones

Rockingham Press

Published in 2000
by
The Rockingham Press
11 Musley Lane,
Ware, Herts
SG12 7EN

**British Library Cataloguing-in-Publication Data**

A catalogue record for this book
is available from the British Library

**ISBN  1   873468 73 3**

Printed in Great Britain
by Biddles Limited, Guildford

*Printed on Recycled Paper*

*To the memory of*
*Richard and Kenneth*

# Contents

*

## Acknowledgements

I would like to thank the editors of the following magazines, journals and anthologies, who have published some of the poems in this collection:

*Smith's Knoll, Envoi, Blade, New Fire, Other Poetry, New Writing, Journal of Contemporary Anglo-Scandinavian Poetry, Sean's House, Lead into Gold, A Marvellous Collection of Birds, Precise Angles of Light, Freedom is a Dangerous Word* (an Amnesty International anthology) and *The Truth is out There.*

"Deposition" won first prize in the Trewithen Poetry Competition 1995; "Pharaoh's Tomb" won first prize in the Envoi Poetry Competition 1996; "Broken Glass" was runner-up in New Writing Competition 1997; "Her Barefoot State" won second prize in the Envoi Poetry Competition 1998; and "Ice Garden" won the A.A. Sanders Poetry Prize 2000.

I would also like to thank David Perman, who published this collection, and Anne Ridler, James Harpur, Viv Grant and John Latham for reading the manuscript.

# 1.

# CAPTIVE BUCCANEER

Animals are not brethren; they are not underlings. They are other nations caught with ourselves in the net of life and time, fellow prisoners of the splendour and travail of the earth.

Henry Beston

# HARE AND SIXPENCE

I rubbed steam from the glass
with a damp fist, expecting
the usual rough sketch of bones and flesh
tied loosely together in a skin bag.

Instead, a hare lay quietly in her form
on the edge of an oatfield,
her eyes startled and wide,
flecked with night's secrets,
rimmed with stars.

She turned away to crouch
at a shallow pool
and sip at the moon.

The sixpence in my hand turned black.

# CAPTIVE BUCCANEER

Somewhere pain is:
I follow its black tug
to a patch of bluebells
netted tight against deer.

Stricken acrobat,
captive buccaneer,
snake become stick
lies motionless,
enmeshed by netting
from golden head to tail.

A bronze eye stares unblinking
as, with kitchen scissors,
I slowly unpick the net.
Night huddles on my back.

First I release his head
clamped and scored by thread:
his tongue flickers like a hazel twig
scenting water, lashes at my hands.
He means business and
I am afraid.

Around his belly, a muddle
of many-layered netting.
Indestructible.
A frog snatched from my pond
bulges in his middle, like
a wooden toadstool in a sock.

Cautious snips … frenzied wriggles
when, half-free, he darts under nettles,
is lost in a rustle of bracken and weeds
wearing his fetters of green nylon.

# *PREY*

A smell, thin and wild as the scream
of a snared hare, seeps through the room.
Something strange has come to stay with us.

Tufts of fur in my cat's claws. A mound
by the hole where he dragged her in alive.
She lies still as a stone, the size of my hand.
Four weeks old and new to the hunting fields.

Peat-brown eyes look through me, unblinking,
as I ease the pipette into her delta-shaped mouth.
Honeyed water dribbles into her fur.

Back in her box, she scrabbles deep
into her nest of wool and hay,
her back paws muddling the saucer
of untasted apples and oats.

I leave her to darkness. Next day I find her
stretched out as if eager to leap from her burrow
and dance in the rising sun.

# THE DOE

I remember the doe
who cropped my roses
one June dawn
when mist hovered over the valley.
It was the way she raised her head,
watched me trustfully, munching on.

I hoped it was she who lay sleeping
on my path next summer,
head resting in a patch of ferns,
hooves in mud.
All day she did not move.

A man with leather gloves
dragged her to the spinney,
chucked her in a ditch,
brushed his hands
then drove away.

Next morning her body
had been sucked like an egg:
entrails glowed shot silk
in the torn pelt.
Ribs shone ivory.

Today I found just
one small, dry bone
in a patch of bluebells
stretching to the sun.

# STICK ROPE DRUM

Villagers have gathered for their
weekly entertainment: time to relax.
The men chew betel nuts, spit out the husks.
Excited children crouch by a broken wall,
among refuse.

They are watching an art form:
the gypsy who leads his bear Gangaram
is proud of his skill.
He holds himself erect as he tugs the rope,
chafes the oozing wound,
beats the drum faster and faster,
deaf to the tortured bear.

A woman in a crimson sari peers over
her husband's shoulder.
She is fond of the bear.
The good luck charms which clink
and jangle round her slender wrists
are made from claws wrenched
from his paws when a cub.

The drumbeat spins around his head;
he watches the stick,
the stick which waves and beats,
waves and beats his rancid fur.
Drops from his wounded snout
fall like tears into his lice-ridden pelt.
Flies round his eyes torment Gangaram,
broken by starvation,
his powerful teeth now blackened stumps.

The men grow restless: time to eat.
Women slip away, drag the children home.
Laughter dies, the show ends.
The gypsy salaams and smiles
as rupees fall at his feet.

He leads the bear to a stout post,
tethers him with a rope so short
Gangaram can neither stand nor lie,
but crouches in a vice of pain.

# DEPOSITION

A russet rag drifts
from a barbed wire fence
where a vixen with oozing dugs
and a hole near her heart
has been hung.

Runnels of black blood
have stiffened her paws,
muzzle and white bib.
Her mouth is a rictus of pain.

Such thirst in death:
her tongue has been lapping
mirages of puddles and streams.

A stink of decay.
*Smelly old thing,* you mutter,
tipping her onto the grass.
Nesting birds have plucked bare
her somersaulting back.

Neat black paws clench downwards
like a ballerina's bloody points.

# BADGER

It is dusk in the wood.
We sit cramped and cold behind trees.
The two hours' wait has made us tetchy.
We are signalling to go home,
give up for the night,
when slow and majestic
he emerges from his sett.
A white blaze on his mask
shines like a shooting star
in this secret world of shadows.

His head sways from side to side
like an ancient god-king
presiding at some holy ritual.
Sniffing the air, he lifts a paw
from the moist earth,
creating silence from the heart of music.
Just two strides away, I watch
this powerful muscle poised motionless
as a harebell in the cleft of a rock.

This same paw digs stones and roots,
can rip apart a dog; curls round newborn cubs,
then rolls them down the bank in play,
scoops up an earthworm; can toss a mole in the air
then scrunch it whole.
Tonight he snuffles and scratches,
turns a log for grubs.
Then suddenly, upwind, the obscenity of man.
Imprinted memory of dogs, the spade, the tongs,
the stink of blood and death.

He melts back into his dark world.

# 2.

# GREENFINGERED DWARF

"I believe so many impossible things," said the Red Queen to Alice.

Lewis Carroll

# ICE GARDEN

I begged him for a garden,
hollyhocks and delphiniums.
He gave me grottos of ice.
No birds sing here: only the sound
of moonlight dreaming snow at midnight.

I have become bone carved from ice.
I spin on a needle's point,
watched by an angel huddled
in snow with icebound wings;
his stricken face as I twirl and twirl.

Those dark and subtle hands
have locked me in this kingdom,
this palace of death-white ice.
Floors are as slippery as his lies.
I wander through cubes of refracted light where

indigo and jade dance on my silver dress,
turn into birds of paradise.
But today a small brown bird
perched on my wrist, then
gave me a pomegranate seed
from his beak.

# EATING PEARLS

I shimmer and dart along terraces of water
which fall and rise with the restless salt tide.
I evade men's deadly nets.

Soft arms and hands have melted
into my ribs, become bony fins.
Legs and feet have fused into my tail.

I swim through gaping eyes
of the silent shipwreck,
whose ghosts gently whisper my name.

Bubbles float from my mouth,
vowels on a heavy page of water.
I eat pearls prised from tight cradles.

I flick, twist and turn
my fish-body in my new element,
the swaying, dim and speckled sea.

# A RING OF STONES

The healing place is a ring of stones
where my father lifts an axe to fell
an ash tree hung with golden fruit.
He has the strength of a pedigree bull.

My mother dances a matador's dance,
teases the bull with a bloodstained cloth.
She hides her face behind a veil
woven from dust and linnet's feathers.

My brother drifts in a purple hammock,
swings between two stones: plays chess
against himself but always loses.
We do not speak. Nobody speaks.

I am a young goat chained to a pole
bleating with terror, with hunger, with thirst.
My father stops chopping the tree. My mother
stops dancing. My brother picks up a knife.

# MAD TROMBONE

On a night when the wind
was breaking the neck of the woods,

when a parrot, a lizard and seven cats
slept hugger-mugger in a flowerpot,

when the test match score
made England blush bright red,

when I waited a second week
for your letter on the mat,

when my toes curled with longing
to dance with you all night,

when the television threw snow
all over *Gardener's World*

and my neighbour phoned to say
a mad Buddhist had burnt down

their museum of model aeroplanes,
when a blind bumble bee hit a daisy

WHAM-BAM and knocked itself out cold,
that very same day I decided

it was time to travel abroad.

So I picked up my *Pianta di Venezia*
where the Grand Canal meanders

like a mad trombone spawning young
all over the page, or like the twigs

and branches of a stricken tree,
or like the large intestine snaking

through the body of a replete man,
or like the blood vessels which burst

in your eye when you asked me to ...

## *THE ISLE OF WIGHT*

is made of white clover
where the bride teeters
on spindly heels of platinum
in her dress woven from cobwebs
tough as a bullet-proof vest
worn by veterans.

The aisle is wide as a meadow
where cows plod towards a stream,
ice-cold, rising from a cave
in the Mendips where smugglers
gloat over hoards of amethyst,
silver and unicorn horn.

Her bridegroom is a tailor's dummy;
she doesn't realise it yet. She will.
He has a sawdust face under a smiling mask
and a white polystyrene body.
He is kitted out with a wedding suit
of the finest raw silk.

His tie is blood-red
and matches his nails.

# GREENFINGERED DWARF

A dark tunnel stretches endlessly through a narrow street
as I grope past dustbins, broken bottles, tins,
then glimpse a chink of light from a shrouded building.
I run through an open door to safety.

Beyond the door lies a courtyard drenched by a harvest moon –
a rich melon globe and I want to eat a chunk of it.
Peering beyond this cool landscape,
I discover a bronze door in the farthest corner.

Blazing, I kick at it, then discover Mystery.
A space in bright sunshine encloses granite walls.
Above stream planets formed from debris, dust and vapour
when the sun was heaving into life.

A flute, fountains rustling like taffeta into alabaster basins.
Mountain water cools my blood, freezes my hands.
This is a garden fit for a magus no less,
a place of spells and magic.

Past a dazzling magnolia to a lemon grove,
a dwarf beckons me, cuts open
a fresh lemon with green hands
which I notice without surprise.

More magic, more spells as I suck the fruit
which tastes of anything I like: suchi, vinegar, albatross,
tadpoles, lavender, kumquats, elderflower.
Nothing as expected, good or bad.

"Goodbye, goodbye, greenfingered dwarf," I cry,
then enter a changed landscape, chill and forbidding
where leaves fall like tears. Ice chains the stream,
the fountain freezes into icicles.

A whirlwind blows faster, faster, sweeps round me
striped fish, turnips, eagles' feathers,
spinning top, shredded sails, singing monkeys.
Harsh clamour as saucepan lids clang together.

"What are these made from?" I ask the whirlwind.
"Tin from the deepest mine," it replied, "where children
 crouch in passages, drag stones for miles."
"Shame on you, shame, shame, shame," the stunted children cry.

## EQUINOX

Noon. Equinox,
when day and night
wrestle together
but neither budges.

The square is as silent
as the birds. No-one about.
Even the dust is still
in the amber heat.

All I see is a white road
empty of ghosts:
we are poised between
shadow and sun,

when the peddler
with his crooked pack
stands, invisible
by the fountain.

# 3.

## DANCING ON BONES

I saw Eternity the other night
Like a great Ring of pure and endless light.
    All calm, as it were bright,
And round beneath it, Time in hours, days, years
    Driv'n by the spheres
Like a vast shadow mov'd, In which the world
    And all her train were hurl'd.

Henry Vaughan

# A NAVAHO SAYING

*"The word that falls on paper seems to stop breathing."*
So where does life begin, if it ends on the page?

With the dry rustle of bats' wings in a cave
as they flitter into daylight or with
the cooling warmth of the newly dead
as their last breath rattles from their lungs,

disturbs a feather on the pillow?
Where the sculptor weighs a stone
or the astronomer hears the first steady pulse
of radio waves? Or where a tormented child

plays at last and the baited bear grubs
for wild honey in the wood?
Is it where we yawn and stretch, amble round
our room barefoot, dry out bay leaves,

thyme and sage hung from an iron hook
and feast on runner beans and raspberries?
Does life begin in a large and once-beautiful house
piled hugger-mugger with mildewed books,

threadbare carpets, broken chairs? If so,
let's tip them onto a bonfire. When the flames have died,
come back to the house, sweep out every nook and cranny
till it overflows with light,

with the murmur of past lives.
Only then may we hear the chink of the bucket
drawn from the well we plunder
time and again in our thirst.

# INVASION

Of course we turned them out,
burned their hovels, built our town
on their land.  I was ordered
by Claudius our centurion,

to dig a rampart of earth
to fend off the barbarians.
Phew, how these Dumnonii stink,
crawling from their thatched homes

like cockroaches.  Can you believe it,
sheep and cattle all live together
in their dark, dirty huts?
Their men sweat in the field,

dig up tin from their mines,
then sail to Gaul in their crude boats
trading for wine and grain.
They stare at us, amazed

at the marble statues of our Gods,
gape at our togas and hypocausts.
Our mighty Empire shows them how to live –
our brick houses, our well-planned streets

– miracles to their gawping eyes.
Claudius found a local girl to his taste,
has settled down with several brats.
Jove's blessing on him – I'm for Rome!

# PAGAN HARVEST

*in mem. Saint Sidwell A.D. 685*

I watched her as she passed my hut each day,
pitcher in her hand. Straight-backed, lithe,
any man would take her as his wife.
Good broad hips for bearing sons.

Then she'd bend over the stream,
her trusting eyes and hair rich
as her father's harvested wheat
gazed back at her from the clear water.

My son, Aleric, took a fancy to the girl,
wooed her hard, even sacrificed a prize bull
to win her. But she favours a new kind of god,
rejects ours, hates our statues and our killings.

The murmurs grew, her father's labourers
hatched a plot to please their master,
left the hayfields carrying scythes,
followed the girl to the stream by the east gate.

Aleric struck first – he had the right, after all.
She fell like a swathe of new-mown grass
over her broken pitcher. They say forget-me-nots
grow red by the stream to this day.

# MAD MATILDA A.D. 1249

How dare they disturb my holy ways
with their banging and cursing, as they build
this folly, this bridge? A profane, vain
useless labour.

I watch them, their trinkets jangling,
laughing, chattering false, idle words
while I pray, hidden in my cell,
for their souls' salvation.

Fire ... flame ... burn, burn.
I am burning as He calls me
to build His house
in the path of Mammon.

No-one will dare move me, lest God's wrath
destroys them, kills their cattle, strikes their home.
Burn ... burning. I am God's instrument
a-flame to do His will.

Now it is finished, the last arch in place,
the cobbles spark-bright on the bridge.
I have built my wattle cell,
blocked their way. It is God's will.

# ONCE UPON A TIME

Squire heaves a bulging rump from his shooting stick,
counts soft and bloodied bodies in the keeper's bag.

His lady-wife sprawls a silk skirt across cold grass,
jabs her parasol at an errant thistle.

From the gaping nursery windows, laughter
dies away in a thicket of ivy.

The under housemaid bangs the coal scuttle
in the invisible grate, wipes soot over her thin cheek.

The cook sweats over a twelve-course dinner,
sturgeon, venison, sugar swans, syllabub.

A barn owl's chick hoots from the deserted stables,
as he waits for his dangling mouse.

In the drained pool, a battered mermaid
gapes at the ghost-pike's murderous grin.

# THE GIFT

Here's my gift: a new heart, a sturdy heart,
its four chambers swept and garnished
with white and purple iris
heaped in silver lustre jugs
under windows opening onto hills
and a clear river white with sails;
all ready for me as I reach you
at last, after a long journey
through rough hill-country,
as I trudge in with muddy boots
and a rucksack filled
with dried apricots and rye bread,
brandy and home-made sloe gin;
a well-thumbed map which smells of garlic,
a compass with needle set true north
and, hidden in one canvas corner,
the swelling chrysalis of an Emperor butterfly.

# *DRAGON*

It is more than I can carry in my hands,
spilling over the rim of the cup
on the way to your house where
you asked me to a meal
served in your cool courtyard
under a full moon.

Our silken knees touched lightly
as the geisha girl served us
saki and mulberries.
Our mouths were purple;
shadow-moths speckled your face
as they fluttered round the carved jade oil lamp.

The dragon under the mountain
yawned, stirred and shook the earth
as we lay together so closely that
the lemon-scented air could not pass
between our bodies, but moved
over our damp skin like silk.

One-legged storks
slept on your reed roof.
All night I listened for the dragon.

# THE ARCHITECT'S HANDS

See the clipped nails, moon-shaped cuticles
a touch of ink on the index pad
I never could scrub out.

Feel the brush between thumb and finger
conjuring shimmering beauty
from marble, gold and lapis lazuli.

The Empress' tomb
reflected in wavering water,
created from desperate grief.

The Emperor's reward ...
elephants laden with jewels
poured like sunlight at my feet.

Then his festering fear
I might create another miracle
surpassing this.

So, today, came his dreaded command.
He allows me a few hours
to caress my wife, pick some lemons,

stroke my child's bright hair.
For the last time,
I shall peel a nectarine

before his swordsman comes
and lifts my hands
onto the royal block.

# SLAVE TRADE

a slash of sunlight
in a twilight room
where green shadows flow

with a crack the skin
breaks and I taste
meadowsweet pith

the casing splits
peels down the flesh
like nylon down a plump leg

as I munch
a turquoise parakeet screams
seed pearls shift on sand

palm leaves flap
like elephant ears
on the trail of water

black bones in chains
fretted by the tide
knock against my memory

# LOST ROOMS

Sun hugs me, yet the house strikes chill.
I search and search, but cannot find
those lost rooms of my dream
which lingers after dawn.

Yet this is my home,
where my first cry
struck the rim of the stars,
made them sing.

Somewhere lives the nursery
with walls blue as a thrush's egg;
an iron grate sparkles with flame
through cough-wracked nights.

A jack-in-the-box grins
as the child bangs his fists
against the window,
drums his heels on the stained floor.

I creep up the attic stairs
past gurgling cisterns
to an oak door.
The rusty key won't budge.

Inside, hang blue and gold rugs.
Scrolls in ivory cases
stand on cedar shelves
with a minstrel's harp.

A marionette swings gently
by a broken fan.
Fragile silks rustle
with the moth's wing.

This room is as startling
and warm as the smile
from a long-dead friend
met in a faraway land.

# VIA NEGATIVA

Jaunty straw hat lies on the table
by a vase of grasses and pink campions.
Scent of lavender, vines and olives
wafts from its plaited brim.
But you are absent ... the house is void,
empty of tea and laughter,
the cassock's swish
displacing living air.

Absent too, those precise hands
adjusting books and papers:
absent the passion which
inscribes love's calligraphy
on broken minds and hearts.

# A LITTLE NIGHT MUSIC

my house weaves music
round me while I sleep

stones sigh stir and settle
old bones on the earth

the dry cough of floorboards
as weightless feet pass by

skinflakes from the dead
settle in my lungs

blot up the day's wet ink
a rose taps a secret code on glass

but down the stairs beyond the lintel
I hear the clack of the treadle

hiss of spit on iron
the soft swish of a fallen dress

clatter of clogs on the flags
a sighing fall of ash on the hearth

# BLINDFOLD

The gentle cropping of your breath,
the band of bone around my ribs.
I am both ship and sea, rudder and sail.
I am air and glass, the wavering flame inside.

Single blue sail flaps on a green pond,
slices tight against the wind:
smack of water on the bow,
shock waves over my hands.

I am giant to this Lilliput boat
shoved across a weed-infested pond
where mottled ducklings swim.
I am four-and-a-quarter.

I am shingles and angles,
the hit of iron and the slap of weed.
Flame curves around glass and is safe
from the amber wind of the North.

# HOUSE OF WATER

Earth's singing tongue is silent,
cut from the hill's mouth years ago.
We walk along a shady path
and shiver as the north wind's
bony fingers fumble
at our clothes:
winter's wolves
snap at our heels.

Between dry banks
slabs lie pinioned
by a tangle of brambles.
The canal is void.

We have emptied its purse,
spilled its silver coins.
Painted narrow boats
have chugged away
to lie like cut roses
in another house of water.

# PHARAOH'S TOMB

*in mem. John Rapp*

Will there be time
to leave the shrouded house,
cross the darkening stream,
to where my father crouches,
mending a stone wall?

He wears shoes with broken toes
(kept for messy, outdoor jobs)
and rumpled flannels tethered
with blue binder twine.

I pass him the trowel and watch
as he dabs mortar on stone
as delicately as a woman
dabs varnish on her nails.

He weighs, balances, cuts
the facets with a neat clunk
of the hammer, then slides
the last stone into place:
like the final block
which sealed the Pharaoh's tomb
until profane hands
looted its treasure.

Will there be time
to gather up the tools,
brush the path clear
of sand and chippings,
amble back to the house,
laughing about the Morris 8
he built from scratch
with those same scholar's hands
which inscribed Greek
with scrupulous love?

# DEATH OF A WOMAN
# MOUNTAINEER 1893

In these last hours,
hold me like a bird
in your hands:
just as my babushka
used to rock me by a log fire
in those Siberian winters
when the snow piled high
against the shingled roof and
we wore wolf furs day and night.

That was my first taste of killing cold,
when people froze to death,
like the lame packman we found
on our path one morning.
He'd crawled towards the candlelight
and fireglow of our house,
selling lace and bone buttons,
love potions and clothes pegs
which lay scattered in the snow,
beyond the reach of his stiff,
outstretched hands.

On those winter nights,
Father would lift his balalaika
from the wall and play in the firelight
while Mother held me safely on her lap,
tapping her feet.
The others sat cross-legged on the floor
watching shadows flicker across the ceiling,
white from the snow-filled forests.

Who are you?
Have you really come to rescue me?
You look like my father,
wearing bearskin boots.
Look – the gleam of his hunting knife –
or is it the glint of ice?
How strong he was.
I know he would lift me
up and away to safety
from this frozen ledge
where I watch my labouring breath
melt little holes in the snow.

How did I fall?
Hard to remember exactly,
but breathless, heart pounding,
I reached the mountain's summit,
then slipped as I turned back.
Exhaustion? Carelessness?
It makes no difference now.

Something shadowy and malign
beckoned me as I fell down,
tumbling from the rock face
until this narrow ledge caught me fast.

Here I lie, dreaming of my dancing days
when I floated in muslin and chiffon
down the marble stairs. Then I was driven
to our neighbour's ball in a troika
across hard-crusted snow,
wrapped in my ermine cloak.

I danced till the stars faded, dawn broke.
Ah yes! That young officer, eyes blue as the sea,
who held me in his arms for waltz after waltz,
but then, with a click of his heels,
left me forever.
He lies cold under snow now,
but I still long for his touch
to warm my frozen, broken body.

Bring me my ermine cloak
and wrap me up against the cold.
Is that a troika I hear?
Yes, there's the ponies' harness jingling.
But why is the snow turning black
and mountains fall on my head?
Hold me ... hold me ...
surround me with tulips, roses
and bougainvillaea ...
offer me schnapps in a silver goblet
to warm my dying blood
but come quickly, oh! come quickly.

# THE EAR

Vincent paces the yellow floor
exuberant with Provençal sun.

He remembers Theo, bills,
his mistress, his quarrel with Gauguin.

Is sharply hungry for a meal,
aubergines and peaches. Muscatel.

As the church clock strikes eleven,
he listens for the thunder,

watches rooks fly in agitation
over stooks of corn.

He puts his razor to his ear.

# HER BAREFOOT STATE

*for Anita and David Wright*

The townsfolk whispered you weren't quite normal –
the way you always wore white,
rarely went out but flitted round the house
like a rare bat in a desert cave.

They couldn't understand why you didn't marry,
like other girls in Amherst,
do the normal thing, bear children,
make antimacassars for the church bazaar;

go visiting on Wednesdays and Fridays
driven in a trap by a piebald horse.
Rumour had it that you couldn't even bake a pie,
never mind sew a patchwork quilt.

No: your lightning struck in a different place.
Secretly, day and night, your spirit fizzed
with poems like sparks of electricity
in a summer's storm. A child's game.

*Do my poems breathe?* you wrote to Higginson.
Not so much breathe as leap, skip, sing,
jump and dance in the passionate landscape
of your soul; never still, never sleeping. You explained:

*I am small like a wren.  My hair is bold,*
*like a chestnut burr and my eyes the colour of sherry*
*left in the glass when the guests have gone.*
I longed to glimpse your ghost, so I travelled

twelve thousand miles to your home hidden
from the highway humming with stretch limos.
That day Amherst wore white, like you.
I slithered through ice and grubby snow

to your house. The windows were shuttered fast,
the garden a white emptiness. On the locked gate:
*Emily Dickinson's home closed for repairs.*
*We apologise for any inconvenience to visitors.*

# JOHN THORNTON, INDUSTRIALIST

I will break you
on the rock of my fist
if you defy me,
by strike or uprising.
My will is the piston driving
this world of steam and steel.

My pulse beats to the rhythm
of the factory whistle,
the clatter of clogs on cobbles
clang and screech of iron gates,
a sluice for the flood of working men.
I control the tide.

I walk through furnace and flame,
both law-giver and judge in my kingdom.
My men joke about me, say my heart
has become a box of rattling coins.
I ignore their snarls and use words
as sparingly as sovereigns.

Because they're wrong, you see.
My granite house on the north wall
of the factory yard
has every comfort I can buy
for my mother's happiness.
Though she does say she misses the sun.

# 4.

# THE CHERRY TREE

We do not become enlightened by imagining figures of light, but by making the darkness conscious.

C.G. Jung

# GLORY GLORY ALLELUIA

Shadows limp across the plain,
pale candle flames in the mountain's shadow.
A scarlet captain sags on his shrunken horse,
his dog scavenges for bones.

Scorched fields, gaping roofs, carcasses
as they straggle through the deep south,
pass a man and wife sprawled in the doorway
locked in death's cold handcuffs.

Charred timbers smoke still;
in the silence, the click of rats' nails.
Sun sandpapers their eyes and skin
and famine hunches over their shoulders

as the saints come marching in.

# ARMISTICE DAY

Let's suppose that all the mouths
of all the men, women and children
who died, unripe, in war,
gathered together on a mountain top in,
let's say, Tibet, and opened wide,
wide as the sky, their beseeching mouths,
what then?

What sound would they make,
and would anyone listen?

Would their sound be the padding
of a wolf's claws across a dark forest floor?

or waves in a fathomless cave?
or the slow opening of a sunflower

to the sun, so that a bullfinch
might peck ripe seeds and live?

Or the soft rustling of a crocodile baby
held safe in his mother's mouth?

# ON THE RAMPAGE

*So they gathered in the house of prayer*
*and there the sword found them and fire devoured them*
*and so they gave themselves as a peace-offering to their God.*

The Prague Pogrom, 1391

In the light of the Passover candles, a drop of red wine
slid down Isaac's beard, trembled, splashed onto the floor.
Shouts, running feet on the cobbles.
Christians on the rampage.


He led his family out.
Dark shapes creeping from cramped houses
into the refuge. The rabbi rose, settled his fringed shawl,
intoned the Kaddish, his voice steady
as shouts and running feet
drew closer.


His wife rocked their baby daughter,
their elder son stroked the baby's cheek.
Other families huddled against the walls,
listening as fists beat against the door
and pitiless feet kicked it down.


The mob stormed into the synagogue,
but the rabbi never faltered.
John the chandler hacked him as he stood
quiet as Christ before Pilate,
slashed at the fallen body,
killed the wife and children.
The synagogue became a butcher's shop,
sticky with blood and entrails,
where Jews lay sprawled in heaps.

Andrew the cordwainer fetched live coals.
They set fire to the floor and to the beams,
they set fire to the tabernacle and to the altar,
they set fire to the Jews, the dead and the dying.

## *FAMILY LIFE IN WAR AND PEACE*

It is one thing to fly abroad for a holiday,
but another to flee your home in a tractor and trailer.
It is one thing to pack your suitcase with novels and sunsuits,
another to abandon everything except two bikes, bedding and
water.

It is one thing to watch your father grow old with dignity,
but another to find him tying a noose round his neck in the
shed.
It is one thing to watch your children play tag in the square,
but another to see your son's foot blown off by a shell.

It is one thing to sow and harvest your crops,
but another to have mines plough your fields.
It is one thing to chat to your neighbour in the street,
another to know he has burnt down your home.

It is one thing to watch the news, then write a poem:
it is quite another to be the people who suffer such things.

# MY BROTHER'S HAT

All that was fifty years ago.
Today I found his toddler's hat in a trunk
studded with brass nails
forming his initials.

Moths had nibbled at the wild flowers and
the birds embroidered by our mother.
A mouse had nested in the crown.
It smelt of decay and loss.

And I remember the other hat he wore,
as smartly brushed as his high black boots
when he goose-stepped through the Polish towns.
The bird crushed by his heel in the gutter.

But, I wonder, when the jeers had died down,
when the court had reached its verdict,
how did he feel when he faced the firing squad,
blindfolded, bareheaded?

# MIDSUMMER'S EVE

A young child twirls patterns on the grass
under an apricot moon.
Trees weave shadows over her white dress as she chants:

> *I love singing to my daughter,*
> *I love singing to the trees.*

> I hear the thin scream of a scar
> as blood gathers fullness and falls.

Flambeaux flicker in the darkness
light our path home.

> Iranian children march onto minefields,
> melt into the sun. I see their scattered
> confetti on the battlefield.

On the steps of a sundial we sip
moon-cooled wine, eat our fill of salad and fish
in the white garden glowing with scent.

> Into a manacled cell a jailer shoves
> a heap of grapes. The hostage shuffles
> in ecstasy, but cannot eat.

I feel the stamp of his beaten soles,
I hear the thin scream of a scar
as blood gathers fullness and falls.

The child, confetti-dappled, sings on:

> *I love singing to my daughter*
> *I love singing to the trees.*

# JILL'S HOUSE

This is the acorn
which dropped to the ground
which sprouted a stem
which grew to an oak,
was felled in its prime
to fashion the beams
which held up the roof
which guarded the home
               that Jill built.

Hers are the hands
which kneaded and sewed
which planted the beans
which laid the floors
which painted the walls
which brewed and spun
which polished the chairs
which sharpened the knives
               that Jack threw.

Jack's was the axe
which hacked the crack
which battered the roof
which broke the beams
which ripped up the floors
which splintered the glass
which smashed the bed
which blew up the home
               that Jill built.

# INTERNEE

Ninety four years have written
history on her face.
Orange squash dribbles down her chin.
Her hands twitch over an unread paper.
She hunches over her grumbles.

> *A girl with auburn curls*
> *bowls a hoop along gravel paths*
> *which loop through*
> *Kensington Gardens.*
> *She nods to Peter Pan.*

A priest bustles into the chintzy
sitting-room, opens his case with
a sharp metallic click; unpacks linen,
missal and vessels to feed the blind,
the deaf and mad who inhabit this space.

> *A woman in rags*
> *shuffles towards the guards,*
> *pleads for a bowl of rice,*
> *a sip of water.*
> *Is beaten back.*

It is a spring morning. Sunlight exposes
smears and dust, casts shadows of swollen veins
on crippled hands. He lifts the chalice.
The silver flashes like a Japanese sword.
The woman grips my hand in terror,
mumbles the wafer in her slack mouth.

# DEAD DOLL

Mary Parker, my favourite doll,
had a china face and a limp rag body:
was won in a raffle.
Taller than me, I dragged her everywhere
when I was three – and she? –
oh – about a hundred years old.

Mary P. was forcibly fed on acorn soup,
rose petals and dock leaves
stirred briskly with a twig
in a rusty tin can.
My kitchen was a hollow in the roots
of a monkey puzzle tree,
but I never saw the monkeys
though I left them food each day.

At night I tucked up my doll
in a wooden cot by my bed.
Never wailing, unprotesting,
she lay motionless as I kissed
her cold face passionately,
then stroked her blind blue eyes:
I crooned her lullabies.

One bright day I took her to a ball,
myself the band and dancers.
Wild as a hare with joy,
I laughed and sang,
hopped up and down the hall,
twirling Mary P. above my head.
Our skirts swirled round like parasols:
we were princesses – beautiful, beloved.

Then crack! The spell broke
as her china face hit a marble table,
splintered to a thousand fragments.
I buried her, every bit,
in a box among the tree roots.
Grief, a darting fish,
lived in a deep dark pool
for years to come.

A lifetime on, I look down
at my mother's china face
asleep forever in her wooden cot.
I fold a bunch of snowdrops
into those stilled hands which, living,
scarcely touched me.

I kiss those frozen lips.

# THE CHERRY TREE

Our cherry tree child, created
under its dazzling white blossom
as leaves' green shadows
flickered over our warm skin.

In the long, slow months after,
I guarded her as she unfurled
within my womb
like a frond of fresh fern.

Then birth. The shock of her hair –
burnished bronze, just like her
Serbian ancestors, we joked.
Her eyes were periwinkle blue.

Rumours of war's savagery
from across the mountains,
but we felt safe, held fast
by our love's strong bond.

The day they came, I was hanging out the washing.
Stanislav was digging up potatoes –
I make a good rich soup with sieved potatoes
and a pinch of coriander.

Our child lay under the cherry tree,
hands flexing like a star fish,
sturdy legs kicking at the clouds,
our goat munching grass.

Deep darkness fell across the sun.
Two black masks with rifles
kicked down the gate,
ordered us to leave.

I hid our baby at my breast, while
Stanislav shielded us both.
One of the masks snatched her,
threw her against the cherry tree.

Our fledgling lies still,
fallen from the nest.
When they had gone, I cradled
a red emptiness all day and night,

then we buried her fragile bones
beneath the cherry tree.

# BROKEN GLASS

We were a mirror image of each other,
making a new shape from the space
between our faces.

You touched me the way you stroked
the rare silk rug we bought
in the souk in Istanbul.

When your fist smashed through the glass
on Christmas Eve,
I was wearing the scarlet dress,
the colour of ripe poppies,
backless with thin straps
where your fingers caressed my skin
the way you fondled your horse
just before you shot it.

# POOR TOM'S A-COLD

Just as some collect stones,
rough from the mountainside or seashore,
which they churn and grind for days,
until they emerge, jewels,
to wear around their neck:
so I collect beggars.

In Heroes' Square, we listen
to a homily on Hungary's past glory,
stare, daunted, at the rows
of cast-iron kings
black against the morning sky.

An old man with a child's hands
dangling from his wrists
gazes blindly into space, mumbles
to the doll lying in his lap.

Up the steep escalator,
filled with goodies, hugging parcels,
a ghost awaits us:
a wheelchair with a marble face –
some desperate journey
through dark shadows.
We fall silent, offer our leavings,
chinking coins
into his tin cup.

The shop window glitters with garnets set in gold,
Bohemian crystal, vases, trinkets.
Heels click and clatter over cobbles,
level with his outstretched hands,
a face crunched against the battered stones.

A witch on crutches begs for help,
stares mutely at our warm clothes
our well-fed bodies.
Hates.

# MYRA HINDLEY

She lifts a white bone to her mouth,
blows across five black holes
wild notes which echo the keening of curlews.

Iron bars form a grid for words
against the shifting sky: spell out
the moor where secret pits
were gouged away in darkness.

But always, in her dreams,
one white shoe, the size of her hand,
blocks the open door.

Note: *Some primitive tribes believe that if a murderer carves a
flute from the shin-bone of his victim, the music he makes will
appease the soul of the person he has killed.*

# BEVERLY HILLS PICNIC

The smell of suntan lotion and baked canvas
as they lie supine beside the pool, chewing olives,
sipping the best sangria. As he rubs oil on her skin
his voice is like a drumbeat before battle.

The afternoon bursts its seams and leaks away.
*"And this,"* he shouts, *"is final."*
Silence lies like a stone between them, so she
dives time and again into the deep end,

while he floats in shallow water, smiling.
Exhausted, she drags herself to the tiled edge
where he comes and lies beside her. All she remembers
of their last hour together is that the light on his thigh

was like the glint in an eagle's eye
as it swoops on a hare.

# SHADOWS

Waking in an icy cave
in the whimpering dark,
she stumbled to her mother's bed
claiming sanctuary.
*Nightmares again?*
*Let's play at shadows ...*

Three-year-old eyes followed
crooked fingers and thumbs
waving deftly against
the candle-flame.
A monstrous fox loomed on the ceiling,
chased a rabbit to the kill.

She watched it stagger, twitch and die.

# CUT: A JOURNEY

Quick, quick ... pressure, urgency
as she stumbles out of bed
down uneven stairs,
hunches over the seat
dizzy with pain and sickness.
Something real pours from her –
a flood of blood
the wine of blood
her flesh is blood.

> *"No use to you now,*
> *better out than in*
> *just a five-inch cut*
> *the scar soon fades ...*
> *full recovery takes a year."*

His belly touches his desk
he fingers his pad, taps his pen.
She sits on the edge of a leather chair,
her empty pelvis tilted towards the floor,
poised like an egg about to smash.

It is Good Friday.
Sunlight ricochets off the walls
as she cuts open hot cross buns,
butters them thickly, warms them
in the Rayburn as she makes the tea.
Her neighbours arrive, immaculate,
their shining children cheeping,
gaping for food.

> Hot cross buns, hot cross buns,
> one a penny, two a penny,
> hot cross buns.

If you have no daughters,
then give them to your sons.
One a penny, two a penny,
hot cross buns.

She has neither sons nor daughters,
she is neither hot nor cross:
she is cold and empty
as the freezer defrosting.
Heavy clunks of ice
drop into the plastic bowl
as she lies awake.
She is ice and filled with dread.

As the ice on her pond slowly melts,
plump pink fish float to the surface.
She trawls the water,
finds corpse after corpse,
buries those staring eyes;
she dreams of fish
gasping for oxygen
in poisoned water,
trapped under ice.
From Flanders' trenches, she catches
whispers from torn lungs, unheard
amidst shrapnel and shot.
She is pierced by that last cry
whose anguish eclipsed the sun.
She is lost in darkness where
earth is iron, sky is lead.

A soothing voice urges:
> *"Just a little pill to make you sleepy*
> *Swallow it down, there's a good girl."*

They think she's lying on a trolley,
being wheeled along pink corridors
towards the operating theatre,
but she knows she's jumping
on a trampoline of stars,
hitching a ride on the Hale-Bopp comet
higher and higher –
until she somersaults around the moon,
goes out like a light or a rocket.

The rabbit darts in terror
deeper into the barley field
as the whirring blades
chop closer, closer.
He dashes for the hedgerow,
is cut in bits.
His severed paws twitch and twitch
like the stitches in her belly,
like soldiers strung on barbed wire.

        Run rabbit, run rabbit
        run   run   run.

Coming round from the anaesthetic,
she is a frayed tightrope
strung across an abyss;
her head is a top spinning wildly
through the valley of dry bones.
The muffled clapper of her tongue
beats uselessly on the salt cave roof
of her mouth, sucking dryness on dryness.
Silence.
Can these dry bones live?

Her stitched-up body is a big bass drum
the doctor's voice is beating on:
boom boom boom, but she is dumb dumb dumb.
Drips, wires, liquid in and out.
A nurse pulls the drain
from the black grin
of her wound.

She curls up in the hospital bed,
slips down the helter-skelter
of a spiralling shell
until she becomes a speck of sand
on the shore of the first dawn.
That night, moonlight flows through her
like water and moonflowers
move gently behind her eyes.
The dark hole in her body,
her pivot and centre,
her sealed cave,
her black dungeon
lies flooded with light.

At dawn, the sun's golden tongue
licks her face roughly,
nuzzling each curve of eye and ear:
a lioness nursing a wounded cub
wakens her to a new day.

> Dan, Dan, the dirty old man
> washed his face in a frying pan
> tossed a pancake on his head,
> fell down in a ditch
> then woke up dead.

She sees his black shadow
sidle through the door,
loom over her bed,
Dan, Dan, the dirty old man.

Anarchy in the basement,
chaos behind the green baize door.
The sink is blocked.
A sharp plunger presses waste
past raw, cut flesh.
Her body ignites like a petrol can,
explodes in a flame of pain.

A solitary violinist plays
in the burnt-out ruins of La Fenice.
Shimmering waves of music
rinse the blackened walls:
the Phoenix is consumed,
to be reborn from the ashes.

Orpheus wanders with a broken lyre
through the cinders of Dresden, Coventry,
Beirut and Sarajevo but stops dead
at the gates of Auschwitz.
Across the frozen wastes of shadow,
he sees six million heaps of ash,
some small in the hand as a sparrow.
Are not two sparrows sold for a farthing?

Persephone felt like this, she thinks:
a shade lost among shades
passing and repassing darkness
but always searching for the brown bird
bearing a pomegranate seed in his beak.

Three children play at doctors and nurses.
Two grab the baby's favourite teddy bear,
hold down its paws, stuff a towel over its nose.
    *"To put it to sleep.*
    *Daddy showed me."*
With a penknife the boy slits open its tummy,
scatters handfuls of sawdust over the floor.
    *"She can't have any more babies now,*
    *just like my mummy. Daddy's glad."*
The toddler, mother to the teddy,
crouches sobbing on the floor,
her face blotched and pitted with sawdust.

    Baby baby bunting
    Daddy's gone a-hunting
    to fetch a little rabbit skin
    to wrap poor baby bunting in.

As the pear-shaped muscle is chucked
by rubber hands into the incinerator,
her unborn children cry out,
writhe into milk-white smoke,
their atoms lost among the stars and moon.
In anguish she hears their cry
fade into infinity.

Returning home, she explores her garden,
finds a nest of wild rabbits.
Sees the sun reflected in a raindrop
resting in the heart of an Alchemilla leaf –
Our Lady's mantle, spread over
earth's quickening womb.